A Word for an International Student

TEMILOLUWA AKINROYE

This book is dedicated to all international students—past, present, and future. The journey of an international student is a beautifully fulfilling one, and I hope that, as you read, you find the peace and readiness you seek. You are exactly where you need to be!

First published by Temiloluwa Akinroye 2024

Copyright © 2024 by Temiloluwa Akinroye

All rights reserved. No part of this publication may be reproduced, stored or transmitted in any form or by any means, electronic, mechanical, photocopying, recording, scanning, or otherwise without written permission from the publisher. It is illegal to copy this book, post it to a website, or distribute it by any other means without permission.

First edition

ISBN: 978-1-7382018-1-5

Table of Contents

CHAPTER 1 1
   Life as an International Student 1

CHAPTER 2 5
   Conquering Culture Shock: Navigating a New World 5

CHAPTER 3 18
   Breaking the Language Barrier: From Struggle to Success 18

CHAPTER 4 29
   Finding Friendship and Community: From Loneliness to Belonging 29

CHAPTER 5 42
   Navigating Financial Challenges: From Survival to Stability 42

CHAPTER 6 55
   The Art of Networking: Building Connections and Creating Opportunities
   55

CHAPTER 7 74
   Breaking Free from Comparison: Building Confidence 74

CHAPTER 8 88
   The Final Word: Embrace the Journey 88

Daily Affirmations For An International Student 92

Chapter 1
Life as an International Student

Recently, I had the opportunity to ask a few students a simple yet profound question: "Describe the life of an international student in two words." Some responded with, "A life of learning and growing," while others said, "It's a life filled with challenges yet fulfilling." After sifting through all the answers, it became crystal clear that two words can hardly encapsulate the journey of an international student. This path is far deeper and more intricate than it might seem at first glance. Many people think it's all about hitting the books, working hard, and nailing that 4.0 GPA, but let me tell you, that's just scratching the surface. The real journey is filled with highs and lows, tears and smiles, each step— a crucial part of your growth and understanding. Although academic success might be at the forefront of your mind, this adventure is also about discovering who you are, exploring your identity, developing your career, and building confidence.

The Deeper Journey: Becoming a Student of Life

Being an international student isn't just about attending

classes in a different country; it's about becoming a student of life. You're not just adjusting to a new academic environment—there are layers of psychological and societal nuances to navigate. Being a student of life means grabbing every opportunity to learn the life skills that will serve you well in your new environment. You need to learn how to become a valued, inclusive member of society. The beauty of this journey is that once you succeed, there's no place or situation you can't adapt to.

Building a New Life: A Soldier's Transition

The life of an international student is much like that of military personnel transitioning from combat to civilian life. At first, they're thrilled to be back home, but they soon realize that the transition is more complicated than expected. They need to figure out how to find a job, how much the culture has shifted since they left, how to rebuild friendships, and how to establish new relationships. In essence, they need to find a way to be valuable and gain value in their new environment. The same goes for you, the international student. You might initially focus on academic success, but soon you'll realize that there's much more to consider—establishing friendships and community, building both professional and personal relationships, finding housing, dealing with culture shock, and building confidence–and let's not forget about keeping your mental health in check and building financial stability. Remember, as an international student, you're not just studying; you're crafting a new life in a new environment, and that requires effort and proactive thinking.

Turning Challenges into Opportunities

The life of an international student comes with its fair share of challenges, but here's the kicker—these challenges push you out of your comfort zone and help you grow. These challenges might feel negative, but as an international student, you need to see them as opportunities for progress. These challenges are crucial for pushing boundaries and discovering what you're truly capable of. Think of them as keys to unlocking new levels of abilities and skills that you might not even know you possess.

The Power of Intentionality

Approach this journey with intentionality. Success as an international student isn't just about academic achievements. It's about understanding and addressing the psychological aspects, like identity crises and cultural adjustments. Being an international student means you have to hit the reset button on how you think and how you do things. You need to be deliberate about what you need to learn and how you're going to learn it. Don't leave your experience to chance or become complacent about your journey. Seize every waking moment to learn something new, to notice differences, and to find your place in your new society because you are here to make an impact.

Setting Up for Success

This book is here to help set you up for success, guiding you to proactively tackle the common challenges you might face on this beautiful journey. Whether it's building a solid network, advocating for yourself, or making new friends, the key is to be intentional and stay relevant in your new environment. Pushing through these initial challenges will not only make you more successful but will also make you more mature and resilient. The experience of being an international student won't just help you achieve academic success; it will transform you into a well-rounded individual, ready to take on the world.

This journey is exciting and fulfilling, a rich and multifaceted experience—a learn-as-you-go adventure. You're never done learning. The path may be filled with challenges, but those challenges are growth opportunities. Embrace this journey with an open mind and a resilient spirit. Every step you take brings you closer to becoming the best version of yourself. Stay determined, be intentional, and celebrate every achievement along the way.

Remember, you're not just an international student; you're a student of life, learning to navigate and succeed in a complex, ever-changing world.

Chapter 2

Conquering Culture Shock: Navigating a New World

"The day had finally come—the last day of my first year of university in Ghana. I was finally leaving and getting the chance to explore the world. I was going to study in Canada. I had awaited this day like a dog awaiting its owner's arrival. My excitement was through the roof. I thought about the extraordinary life I would live, the culture, the diverse friends I would make, and the goals I would achieve.

When I arrived in Canada at 18, I didn't realize I was stepping into the unknown. Having spent my formative years in Ghana, the move was both exhilarating and daunting. I barely understood what was ahead of me, and when it became my reality, I quickly became clueless about navigating it. Initially, it was fascinating, but as the weeks passed, I received the shock of my life. I went from being excited to completely confused and frustrated. Everything was so different from what I was used to. It was like night and day. "Where do I start?" I constantly asked myself. One of the biggest shocks was realizing the level of independence needed to get things done. Back home, I relied heavily on my parents for support, from helping with school supplies to grocery shopping. In Canada, I realized I had to fend for myself, and the surprising thing was that it was normal for people my age to be already taking care of themselves.

Academically, the differences were overwhelming. In Ghana, the education system was more relaxed. During my first year of studying Business Administration, I didn't need to study intensely to pass my courses. It was basically "cram and go," as people might say from my country. The curriculum was laid out, with specific classes assigned for each year. In Canada, however, I found myself constantly navigating and making decisions. Despite having an enrollment system to guide us, I had to determine which professors to choose and which courses to prioritize. This level of autonomy was a significant adjustment. So much information was available that my mind was constantly overwhelmed and overstimulated. I always had to consider several factors when making a decision. A few weeks into the school year, I struggled to pass some of my papers, leaving me frustrated for months. I was doing everything, including reading every textbook I could find, but it wasn't getting me anywhere. I would be in the library from morning to night, yet my results remained poor. I realized the educational approach was quite different. It was more application-based, demanding a lot of critical thinking and active engagement. It wasn't what I was used to. It wasn't just about memorizing information but applying knowledge practically, which pushed me to adopt a different learning and studying style.

The most challenging differences were in the social norms and cultural practices. Coming from a conservative culture, many *aspects of life and activities I saw were frowned upon. I couldn't understand the concept of asking questions during classes because I was taught it was rude and disrespectful. I was shocked when I realized I had to talk and participate to earn points for my grades in class. My brain couldn't comprehend it—I had never done that before. There were days when I would go back home and cry because I couldn't push myself to ask questions or express my opinions. I missed what I was used to and hated that I couldn't get acquainted with my environment. Everything felt strange and unfamiliar, and I was constantly tired of getting things wrong. I began feeling homesick and less confident.*

My lack of knowledge of social conduct aggravated me, like not knowing what gestures to make during a conversation or what was considered rude. It all left me feeling like I was constantly walking on eggshells.

I grew tired and finally decided to embrace the new system. Whenever I didn't understand why something was the way it was, I wouldn't hesitate to ask questions. I realized that no question is wrong, and it is good practice to express that you are new to the environment so people are more cautious to include you in conversations. I also began researching more about my school, Canadian culture, and its people. I utilized campus resources and counselling services to help navigate the emotional and mental roller coaster. I tried to familiarise myself with people in the diaspora (people who knew a bit about both cultures and systems) to mentor me and help me get acquainted. I would also imitate people's gestures during conversations, and the more effort I put into learning and observing, the less it felt like a burden and more like a part of me. I finally started to understand how the educational system worked, which was reflected in my improved grades. I started utilizing various strategies for studying and applying the knowledge I gained in class. I began to use some of that knowledge in the real world. I finally felt joyful when I could understand some slang in conversations and respond without overthinking. I became more comfortable speaking in class and engaging with my peers. I finally started adopting Canadian culture without the fear of losing my own. This diverse background quickly became a unique strength, allowing me to connect with people on multiple levels."

A girl from Accra, Ghana.

Let's face it–culture shock is one of the first challenges you will encounter as an international student. It's that overwhelming cocktail of confusion, stress, and disorientation that hits you when you're suddenly dropped into a completely new cultural environment. It's not just you— every immigrant, every newcomer, feels it. Why? Because as humans, we build our lives around the norms, food, weather, and systems we're used to. These things become part of our identity, shaping how we see the world. But when you're uprooted from all that familiarity and tossed into a new environment, your mind and body can go into a bit of a meltdown. Suddenly, everything you thought you knew is challenged, leading to a tidal wave of anxiety and uncertainty.

The Roller Coaster Ride of Culture Shock

Culture shock doesn't just hit you all at once—it's more like a roller coaster with different stages. First, there's the honeymoon stage. Everything is shiny, new, and exciting. You're fascinated by the culture, the people, the diversity. It's like being on an extended vacation. But, like all honeymoons, this phase doesn't last. For example, the student in the story was excited about moving to another country and exploring the lifestyle, culture, and people. However, after a few weeks, the frustration stage sets in, marked by anxiety, and confusion. This is where the excitement fades, and reality sets in. Communication becomes a struggle, social norms start to clash, and suddenly, everything that was once exciting becomes a source of stress. Homesickness creeps in, and you start longing for the familiar comforts of home. From the story you read earlier, the student experienced frustration with the school system, social norms, and communication styles, which is common in this stage. This stage can be tough and might last a while, depending on how different your new environment is from what you're used to and how open you are to adapting.

Then comes the adjustment stage. Slowly but surely, you start to get the hang of things. You figure out how to navigate your new surroundings, and life starts to feel a bit more manageable. You develop coping strategies, find resources, and begin to feel more comfortable. In the story earlier, the student tried to learn about her environment and sought resources to help her adjust, eventually becoming more comfortable. Finally, there's the acceptance stage. You've made peace with the differences and learned to function well in your new environment. You might not fully understand everything, but you've found a balance that works for you. The student in our story, for example, was able to blend her Ghanaian roots with her Canadian experiences, turning her cultural diversity into a strength.

The Many Faces of Culture Shock

Culture shock isn't just about missing home; it can hit you in various aspects of your life. First off, there's the language barrier. Struggling to understand and be understood can make you feel isolated and frustrated, making it harder to form connections. Then there are the social norms. What's considered polite in one culture might be seen as rude in another, leading to awkward situations and feelings of embarrassment or alienation. Another challenge is information overload. In the Western world, there's an expectation to be constantly informed and make decisions based on a flood of data. If you're not used to this, it can feel like you're drowning. Without curiosity and proactive inquiry, you might miss opportunities and feel lost in many choices. The student in our story felt overwhelmed and frustrated by the abundance of information needed to make even the smallest decisions.

Educational differences add another layer to this challenge. The educational system is a significant part of how a society functions, thinks, and learns. As an international student, adjusting to new teaching styles, expectations, and assessment methods can be frustrating. In some countries, education might be more structured and less focused on critical thinking, while in others, it demands a high level of independence and problem-solving.

The Emotional Toll of Culture Shock

Culture shock can make you emotionally unstable—it can shake you to your core, making you question everything. You might find yourself grappling with existential questions like, "Where do I even start?" or "What do I really want out of life in this new place?" Social anxiety can creep in, making you second-guess your every move. You may start worrying about being judged, misunderstood, or simply not fitting in. This fear can lead to a vicious cycle—the more anxious you are, the more you pull back, which only heightens your sense of isolation and loneliness. Questions like, "Why did they look at me like that?" or "Am I doing something wrong?" can haunt you, causing self-doubt and insecurity. Misunderstanding cultural cues can make you feel rejected or out of place, further intensifying your anxiety.

But here's the good news—culture shock isn't a life sentence. You can overcome it by shifting your mindset, confronting your fears, and positioning yourself for success. It's all about adaptation. The key is to be proactive—learn the ropes, embrace the differences, and use them to your advantage.

OVERCOMING CULTURE SHOCK

Normalize your experience

Let's start with a reality check: culture shock is completely normal. It happens to everyone, so cut yourself some slack. As an international student, you've made a monumental decision to uproot your life, leaving everything familiar behind to pursue education or a better life thousands of miles away. Of course, you're going to feel out of place, confused, or overwhelmed. That's just part of the deal. Whenever you get frustrated, take a deep breath and remind yourself that this is your first time in a completely new environment, surrounded by a different culture and system. It's okay to find it challenging. You're not alone in this— countless other international students are facing similar hurdles. Even the locals would struggle if they had to move to a different country. So, if you feel lost or disoriented in your first year, recognize that this is just a regular part of the adjustment process. It's temporary, and you will get through it.

Embrace the Learning Curve

You're not going to have everything figured out right away, especially in your first semester or year. There will be times when you think, "Man if only I'd known that sooner!" That's all part of the learning curve. It's easy to look back and wish you'd known more, but remember that everyone goes through a period of adjustment. You're not supposed to know everything right off the bat. Be patient with yourself and trust that you'll gradually learn and adapt to your new environment. Every misstep is just another step towards getting the hang of things.

Don't be too Hard on Yourself

Adjusting to a new culture and educational or social system is a big challenge, and it's perfectly okay to make mistakes or feel uncertain. Think of it like a plane taking off—it takes time and effort to reach cruising altitude. At first, you might experience some turbulence, and it may feel like the plane could plummet, but in reality, it's just passing through the "unfamiliar" clouds and pressure of gravity before stabilizing. Your adjustment process is similar. There will be ups and downs, but with persistence and self-compassion, you'll find your footing. Don't waste time beating yourself up over what you don't know or the mistakes you make. Instead, focus on your progress and the effort you're putting into adapting. Celebrate small victories and milestones, no matter how minor they may seem. This kind of positive reinforcement will boost your confidence and keep you motivated.

Look for resources and get comfortable asking questions

One of the best ways to navigate culture shock and adapt to your new environment is to actively seek out resources and get comfortable asking questions. Don't be afraid to ask yourself, "What do I need to know?" It might be tricky since you're in uncharted territory, but asking questions is key. Find a mentor or friend who understands both your culture and the new environment—someone who can act as a bridge between the two worlds. When I first arrived in Canada, my parents introduced me to their friend's daughter, who was also my roommate. She showed me where to get certain things, how to start conversations, and what behaviours were appropriate. Through our talks, new questions popped up, like where to find specific information or what's considered polite to say. If you've made a friend in class, don't hesitate to ask them about the culture, educational system, and daily life. They can provide valuable insights to help you adjust more quickly.

Many international students come from educational systems where asking questions isn't the norm, and information is provided without inquiry. However, in your new environment, asking questions is crucial. It helps you dig deeper and uncover information that might not be immediately obvious. Without asking, you might miss out on important details and resources, leaving yourself vulnerable to misunderstandings or missed opportunities. Engage with the right people who know the system well and can offer accurate and helpful advice. For example, I struggled with my English essays in my first year because I was using study methods from back home. Then one day, my roommate mentioned the importance of understanding the class objectives and learning points outlined by the professor before tackling an assignment or test. That conversation completely changed how I approached my studies. I asked her why, and she explained that the essence of the class is written in the objectives, and the professor must ensure you have achieved those objectives, which is reflected in your assignments and exams. That changed my entire perspective on my study methods and the answers I was giving in class. Local friends can offer clarity on these things, explaining the educational system's nuances and providing tips on how to study effectively.

Observe and Imitate People During Conversations

Another powerful strategy is to observe and imitate people during conversations. An educational environment is one of the best places to understand how a society works, so use it to your advantage. Immigrants who come as students often find it easier to adapt than those who come as workers because they're constantly surrounded by opportunities to learn the culture. Pay attention to the sounds, phrases, and social cues that locals and students use. Note your observations and try incorporating them into your interactions.

By observing others, you can learn the appropriate ways to engage in small talk, express opinions, and navigate social situations. There's some truth to the saying "Fake it till you make it." While you shouldn't pretend to be someone you're not, imitating successful behaviours can help you feel more comfortable and confident. If you see someone handling a conversation in a way that resonates with you, try using that approach in another interaction. Pay attention to how others react and decide if this new behaviour feels right for you. For example, when I first came to Canada, I noticed that people would say "thank you" or "sorry" in nearly every conversation, even to the bus driver when getting off the bus. So, I started doing it too— and you know what? The bus driver would acknowledge me with a wave. These small gestures might seem insignificant, but in

Canada, they show respect and kindness. If locals often start conversations with small talk about the weather or recent events, try doing the same. It's a great way to break the ice and make interactions smoother.

Be Open and participate in Societal Activities

A big part of adapting to a new culture and environment is unlearning certain preconceived notions and being open to new experiences. We'll dive deeper into this throughout the book, but let's start with this: how things are done in your home country might be vastly different from how they're done here. You need to be willing to unlearn and adapt for a smooth transition.

One effective way to do this is by participating in cultural activities. Engaging in these activities helps you immerse yourself in the local culture, understand its nuances, and appreciate its uniqueness. Whether it's attending local festivals, joining cultural clubs, or participating in university-hosted events, these experiences can provide valuable insights and help you feel more connected to your new surroundings. For example, in Canada, hockey is a big deal. When I first started classes, I'd hear people talk about "the game last night," and I'd be completely lost. Over time, I realized that hockey is a major part of Canadian culture, and knowing a bit about it would help me engage with people at school or work. Now, I'm a proud fan of the Edmonton Oilers. So, get involved in the cultural practices that matter to the people around you. It'll help you learn about the culture and boost your confidence in interacting with others.

By following these strategies—normalizing your experience, embracing the learning curve, being kind to yourself, utilizing resources, observing and imitating others, and being open to new experiences—you'll be well on your way to overcoming culture shock and thriving in your new environment. Remember, this journey is about growth, learning, and becoming the best version of yourself. So, take it one step at a time, and enjoy the process!

Chapter 3

Breaking the Language Barrier: From Struggle to Success

"It was that time of the year again—the season for university applications. The IELTS (International English Language Testing System) Exam was a requirement for most universities abroad, and as a Chinese kid, you can imagine my greatest fear. I needed a score of at least 6.5 out of 9 points to get straight into university. Unfortunately, I managed only 5 out of 9, barely scraping by. Thankfully, I got accepted to a university on the west side of Canada with one condition—I had to join an English Language School. I was indifferent to the news. How hard could it be to learn English? As the days progressed, my excitement grew, and I eagerly anticipated my departure.

I remember the first time I stepped into my dorm. A wave of excitement and relief washed over me. It felt like I had walked onto the set of a TV show like The Big Bang Theory. Everything was surreal. However, as the days passed and my surroundings became more familiar, what felt like a fairy tale began shifting into a harsh reality. I hadn't realized how much harder it would be—

communication!

Before moving here, I knew I needed to learn English, but it seemed I hadn't accurately calculated the challenges and risks I would encounter. It's just the English language, right? Soon, I found myself too shy to speak, understanding only half of what people were saying. Constant misunderstandings left me feeling like people couldn't take me seriously. I felt stupid like I wasn't smart enough. In this new environment, people often engaged in "small talk," a cultural norm for building rapport. I considered joining these conversations, but second thoughts would constantly flood my mind. Would I be considered an outcast? How would people measure my intellect? I was so scared to speak that I often resorted to non-verbal cues like nodding or smiling during conversations. I couldn't express myself as an educated individual which gradually eroded my identity and confidence. I no longer recognized myself. Was this the same kid from Guangzhou?

Things worsened when I joined my university's English School. What was supposed to aid my performance quickly became a validation of my incompetence. It was rough. During one of my English courses, we were required to write essays to measure our improvement. This was my first time writing in-class English essays. Understanding my limited experience with speaking and writing English, I scheduled time with my professor to seek guidance on my performance. Despite all my efforts, I couldn't get a grade higher than a B-. I revisited my professor repeatedly, expressing my desire to improve. After each session, I implemented their recommendations, expecting better results but at the end of the *semester, I saw no progress. I was desperate for my grades to validate my progress since I didn't see visible improvement in daily conversations.*

Group discussions were another significant challenge. We had Friday group discussions, and I often felt intimidated when students switched to more formal and articulate speech. It made me sick to my stomach. The cycle continued daily until one day, I decided to take matters into my own hands. I quickly understood no one was coming to save me, and I needed to leave my pity party.

Towards the end of my first year, I spoke with a friend who was already taking academic courses. We discussed joining some of her classes to learn more about English and how to engage with it. My English courses were in the afternoon, and her psychology and statistics classes were in the morning, so it worked well. Despite my insecurities, I wanted to immerse myself in the academic environment and find ways to expand my knowledge and vocabulary. At first, it was overwhelming, and I felt scared at times. But after some time, I thought to myself, no one knows me in this class, so I had better concentrate on why I was here. I took note of the words I needed help understanding and asked my friend questions after class.

The more I sought knowledge and exposed myself to English-speaking environments, the less uncomfortable I became. It sparked my interest in learning more about the English language. I stopped speaking Mandarin with my Chinese friends and switched to English. I also started taking my course notes in

English to improve my articulation and writing skills. I was tired of being overlooked and was eager to contribute to conversations and showcase my intellect. Slowly, my confidence grew, and I became less afraid of making mistakes. My mindset shifted—my mistakes didn't define me; my progress did. I realized that the English language did not define who I was.

As I moved on to academic courses, I found ways to be more vocal about my opinions, especially in participative classes, and refused to be intimidated by large vocabulary. I understood I was on a journey and would surely reach my goals."

A boy from Guangzhou, China.

Language barriers are one of the toughest hurdles you'll face as an international student. A language barrier happens when there's a gap in understanding between the person speaking and the person listening.

When you're trying to communicate in a language you don't fully grasp, it affects every part of your life—academically, socially, emotionally, and mentally. Suddenly, something as simple as asking a question becomes a monumental task. Moving from a familiar environment where words flow easily to a place where you struggle to express even basic ideas makes the transition feel like an uphill battle.

The Ripple Effect of Language Barriers

Miscommunication is awkward enough without the added pressure of living in a new country. This often discourages international students from initiating conversations or participating in social activities. You might worry about saying the wrong thing, using the wrong word, or not being understood at all. It's frustrating, but even worse—it can push you into social isolation. And when you stop engaging, your confidence takes a nosedive, making it even harder to connect with others.

Language Barriers and Confidence

In an academic environment, confidence often comes from how well you can express yourself through language. That's a huge challenge for international students, especially those who have an accent or aren't yet fluent in the local language. In many Western societies, the way you speak influences how others perceive your intelligence. This can feel unfair, but it's the reality. People use fancy vocabulary to project competence, and if you can't keep up linguistically, you might be unfairly judged as less capable—even if you're a genius in your field.

Body language is another layer to this challenge. What might be normal or polite in one culture can be perceived very differently in another. For example, in Canada, it's considered polite to smile at people you pass by on the street or while riding the bus. But in other countries, smiling at strangers might be viewed as intrusive or strange. These subtle cultural cues add an extra level of complexity when you're already trying to navigate a new language.

The Identity Crisis Triggered by Language Barriers

Language isn't just about communication—it's about identity. We build our sense of self through words, shaped by what we say and how others perceive us. If you've always been known as the "math whiz" or the "creative writer," you take pride in that identity because it's reinforced by your ability to communicate it. But when language barriers prevent you from expressing your talents or ideas, it's easy to start doubting yourself. Who are you if you can't convey the skills and attributes that define you?

In the earlier story, our student faced exactly this issue. They knew they were intelligent, but struggled to express it in a way their peers could understand. That communication gap led to self-doubt, triggering an identity crisis. If you can't find a way to bridge that gap, you might start believing those negative thoughts—and that's when it becomes a self-fulfilling prophecy.

Prejudice and Language Barriers: Battling Assumptions

Here's another unpleasant truth: language barriers can bring out prejudice. People might unconsciously (or consciously) assume that you're uneducated or unintelligent because of your accent or language proficiency. It's unfair, but it happens. Instead of shrinking under their assumptions, stand tall, extend some leniency and educate them while diligently guarding your identity and progress. Simultaneously, it's easy to start worrying about being judged unfairly, but that mindset can lead you down a dangerous path. The more you stress about being perceived negatively, the more likely you are to act in ways that confirm those unfair beliefs. Rather than seeing yourself as a victim, carry yourself with confidence. Trust me, people are becoming more appreciative of diverse languages and accents, and many will respect you for your efforts.

So, just like culture shock, language barriers don't last forever. You won't always feel this out of place. With the right mindset, a willingness to learn, and the confidence to keep pushing forward, you will overcome this challenge. You've already shown courage by stepping into a new country—don't let a language barrier hold you back.

OVERCOMING LANGUAGE BARRIERS

Enjoy Making Mistakes

I know this sounds like the hardest advice to follow, as an international student, you need to learn to enjoy making mistakes. I get it—many of us come from cultures where mistakes are seen as weaknesses or signs of laziness and sometimes we trick ourselves into thinking that success is all about the results. Well, that is not true. Success is built on the foundation of mistakes. When you're tackling language barriers, the only way forward is by embracing mistakes. Stop seeing them as roadblocks and start treating them as stepping stones. You can't succeed without failing first—period. And trust me, you're going to make a lot of mistakes. You'll mix up words, mispronounce things, or feel like you're not making sense at all. But guess what? It's all part of the process. There's that old saying, "Practice makes perfect," but I like to say, "Practice makes progress." Your goal isn't perfection; it's progress. So find ways to step out of your comfort zone, fumble a little, and learn from it. Challenge yourself by taking that public speaking class or starting conversations in English more often. Remember the person from the story earlier? They began writing class notes in English, and over time, it transformed their articulation and confidence.

Beware of Analysis Paralysis

Now, while embracing failure, don't fall into the trap of overthinking. This is what we call "analysis paralysis," where you spend so much time worrying about every mistake that you never actually move forward. For example, you should not count how many mispronunciations you have had in a day. Obsessing over every little misstep will only tank your self-esteem. One of the biggest challenges for international students is getting stuck in this negative loop, focusing more on failures than on progress. Remember the person from the earlier story? They let the fear of failure stop them from engaging in conversations, and that fear became their reality. Whatever you focus on grows. Focus on progress, not perfection, and you'll see the difference.

Create a Safe Space for Mistakes

Here's another key to making progress—practice making mistakes in a safe environment. Surround yourself with people who support you, correct you constructively, and help you grow without judgment. This could be among other international students, understanding professors, or friends who won't flinch when you stumble over a word. Like the student from the earlier story, they started speaking English with their friends—a safe space where they could get positive feedback and constructive criticism. They even followed a friend to class to learn new words in context. A safe environment makes all the difference. When you feel secure, your confidence grows, and that overthinking voice in your head quiets down, helping you learn with ease. Soon, you'll speak up more and worry less.

Embrace Humility

You've got to be humble enough to ask for help, receive feedback, and—brace yourself—admit you don't know everything. Humility is what lets you ask questions without fear of judgment. When you can say, "I don't understand, can you explain?" you open the door to learning. No one is going to think less of you for it. In fact, people appreciate those who are eager to learn and grow. In *Failing Forward* by John C. Maxwell, the author emphasizes that you've got to get over yourself. No one cares about your mistakes as much as you do. So, if you want to move forward, be willing to fail and learn from your failure. It's the only way to grow.

Appreciate Slow Growth

When it comes to overcoming language barriers, remember that slow and steady wins the race. Learning a language is like climbing a mountain—it takes time, patience, and consistency. This generation loves instant gratification, but guess what? Real progress takes time and no matter how slow your growth is, it is still growth. Just like the slow drop of water will eventually break a rock, your consistent effort will eventually pay off. You may have to put in extra time—attending tutoring sessions or studying longer hours and although you might feel like you're not catching up as fast as your peers if you keep pushing, your hard work will pay off. The student in the story you read earlier started attending their friend's academic classes and, while confused and overwhelmed at first, eventually began seeing progress. Consistency was key.

Eliminate Disappointment

The beauty of embracing slow progress is that it helps you dodge disappointment. If you're constantly asking, "Why haven't I mastered this yet?" you're only setting yourself up for frustration. That kind of disappointment clouds your judgment and prevents you from thinking clearly. When you appreciate your small wins, you can see the bigger picture and plan your next steps effectively. Take a page from the earlier story. If the student hadn't paused to recognize the progress he'd already made—like experiencing interest and seeing results while attending his friend's academic classes—he wouldn't have been able to come up with helpful ideas to progress, such as writing his class notes in English. It's that positive outlook that helps you think clearly and stay motivated.

Slow growth is still growth, and every bit of effort counts.

Celebrate the small victories, even if they seem insignificant. Those little wins add up, and before you know it, you'll be hitting your goals.

You Are Exactly Where You Need to Be

Lastly, remember this—you are right where you're supposed to be. If you're learning a new language or facing language barriers, know that the practice and effort you're putting in are part of your journey. You might feel overwhelmed or question why things are so difficult, but you're not behind. Use this time to your advantage—maybe start a YouTube channel or TikTok account to document your language-learning journey. Get creative. Work with others who need help with your native language. Embrace where you are, and never underestimate the progress you're making. Soon enough, you'll look back and see just how much you've grown.

Remember, success isn't just about results—it's about the journey, the consistency, and the progress you make along the way.

Chapter 4

Finding Friendship and Community: From Loneliness to Belonging

"I arrived in Canada at the age of 16, full of excitement and anticipation to explore the facets of my new world. Many people thought my excitement was driven by the impulsive thoughts of experimenting in areas of life I had not been exposed to as a teenager, but that was not the case. I was genuinely excited because I had a goal to accomplish: to succeed. Part of this goal was to find a close circle of friends who shared the same values and desire to conquer the world.

Due to my age, my parents were not comfortable with me going straight to university, so they enrolled me in a boarding school in Hamilton, Ontario, for a year. To my surprise, it felt like a home away from home. Many of the students spoke Russian or came from Kazakhstan, making it easy to befriend them. The familiarity of the language and shared cultural background made my transition much smoother. As months went by, I quickly became "that" girl. I had gained many friends rapidly, bonding over shared experiences and similar backgrounds. I felt on top of the world. It was like a dream come true. I was popular and a straight-A student—what more could a girl want? But very quickly, the school year ended, and I needed to make some weighty decisions about which university to attend. This was where the real challenge began.

Most of my international student friends stayed in Ontario, choosing universities within the area. However, due to the high tuition fees and living costs, I had to make the tough decision to move to Alberta for a more affordable education. As I landed in Edmonton, tears began to flood my eyes as I realized I was all alone and needed to start from scratch. The initial comfort I experienced in the prior year was a temporary shelter, and things were about to get real in university. While riding in an Uber to my university dorm, I could barely take in the sight of the beautiful city as tears blurred my vision. "Where do I even begin?" I asked myself. The fear and uncertainty about what this environment could offer consumed my mind. As an international student, I couldn't believe I was experiencing these same emotions and anticipations again. What would people think of me? What are they like? I was filled with so much anxiety. I had no friends and no immediate connections. I knew no one!

My first year of university was a whirlwind, to say the least. Coming from Kazakhstan, a country of 20 million people, I felt like a tiny fish in a vast ocean. I was amazed by the number of people at my school. How could I possibly find friends here? I wondered, overwhelmed by the crowds and busyness. I was an Asian-looking girl who spoke Russian and came from a Muslim background. These diverse facets of my identity made it hard to find a group I could fully relate to. I felt like I had multiple identities and desperately wanted to fit in.

Questions about my identity always ran through my mind: "Where do I fit in? Which community do I belong to?" Despite knowing who I was, I was concerned that people would either put me in one box or no box at all. Slowly, I started to isolate myself, and the wave of loneliness hit heavily. For days, I would not see or speak to anyone, and it began to affect my academics. I went from being a straight-A student to barely maintaining a 2.7 GPA. I even started to question my decision to go into the Engineering field, but deep down, I knew the reason behind my failure. I felt overwhelmed and out of place. My identity crisis and academic failure were eating away at me, and I had no one to turn to.

I spent my entire first year lonely and depressed, with so many soaked pillows and several Fs as evidence of my emotional instability. However, during the summer break, I decided I had to put on my big girl pants. I realized I couldn't continue this way until my fifth year in university because I was never like this in high school or Kazakhstan. Something had to change, and it had to change fast. So, I decided to embark on deep reflection and figure out how to get to know people and surpass my fear of rejection. During this period, I decided to join the International Student Association and the Engineering Student Society in the fall. This was one of the best decisions I ever made.

Slowly, as I got to know people, the more I felt at home. I met other international students who shared the same sentiments and struggles, and we began to bond. I no longer cared about people's opinions of my identity and was very open to sharing various aspects of it. I realized I didn't have to pick one part of my identity over another; they all together made me who I am. Very quickly, I became pretty familiar with the clubs and gained a close circle of friends. People started to recognize me in the hallways and associate me with the programs I organized in school. At this point, I finally found some balance and peace in my life. My grades improved significantly, and there were no longer teary pillows.

While volunteering in these student clubs, I realized that many other international students struggled to find a community and needed a shoulder to cry on. By hearing other students' struggles, my pain slowly transformed into passion. I wanted to be the representation of what I lacked in my first year. As I continued to act on this passion, I built a community for myself and others.

The friends and support network I had dreamt of slowly finally started to become a reality."

A girl from Almaty, Kazakhstan.

As an international student, it's incredibly tough to leave behind everything familiar, pack up your life, and move halfway across the world. You're stepping into the unknown, and let's not sugarcoat it—the need to rebuild your social circle from scratch is downright daunting. Suddenly, you're not just figuring out a new country, but also trying to figure out how to make friends who share your values and interests. It's a lot. We're humans and companionship is essential, regardless of your personality type–and knowing this only makes the process scarier. No one wants to feel alone, and the fear of not connecting with others can be paralyzing. Many times, this overwhelming process leads many international students to face bouts of loneliness, homesickness, and even rejection.

Pervasiveness of Loneliness

Loneliness is a pervasive problem among many international students. Life without your usual crew of friends and family can feel unbearably empty. Moving abroad often means being separated from the very people who used to lift you. And the truth is, the way Western societies are structured can amplify that sense of isolation. The social systems, the fast-paced lifestyle, and the individualistic culture can make you feel like you're on the outside looking in. And when you combine that with the fear of rejection or the feeling that you don't quite belong, it makes connecting with others feel even more challenging. It's easy to find yourself thinking, "Will they accept me for who I am? Will I ever find my tribe?" These questions can paralyze you, making it hard to take that step to join social circles or attend gatherings. When you feel like an outsider, it's easy to convince yourself that no one wants you in their group. So, you retreat further, and that just deepens the loneliness.

The Role of Cultural Identity

When you move abroad, you can't escape the fact that you stand out. You may feel like no one looks like you or no one speaks your language. Suddenly, you're hyper-aware of your differences, and it only intensifies the loneliness. You start wondering if you'll ever find a community that embraces all of you—the parts shaped by your home culture and the parts shaped by this new world you're trying to navigate. Think of a chameleon—it can blend in everywhere, but does it truly belong anywhere? As international students, you often feel like that chameleon, caught between multiple identities. Finding a place where you feel seen and accepted for all that you are can feel nearly impossible, leaving you guarded and hesitant when interacting with new people.

Homesickness and Emotional Roller Coasters

The loneliness and struggle to find your community don't just make you feel isolated—they often trigger intense homesickness. That ache for home is real, and it doesn't go away just because you've enrolled in a new school or found a new city to live in. The absence of familiar faces, places, and comforts can mess with your emotions, leaving you emotionally unstable. You may find yourself constantly thinking of home, of the people you left behind, and that nostalgia can make it even harder to engage in your new environment. On top of that, there's the frustration—wanting so badly to connect, but feeling stuck. That feeling of helplessness, where you want to form relationships but don't know how, can lead to an emotional tailspin. Homesickness, nostalgia, anxiety, and even depression can creep in, building a wall between you and the very people you're trying to reach. It's an emotional whirlwind that makes it hard to trust, to open up, and to truly settle in.

In the end, the process of adapting to a new country and building a support system is complex. It's not just about making friends—it's about finding a place where you can be your full, authentic self. It's tough, but you can do it. Keep going—you'll find your people.

OVERCOMING LONELINESS AND BUILDING COMMUNITY

Love Yourself

Loving yourself is foundational to navigating the whirlwind of building friendships and community as an international student. Loving yourself means accepting who you are—your identity, your struggles—and embracing your current journey, no matter how bumpy. It's easy to be harsh on yourself, complain about loneliness, or stress over not making friends right away. But here's the hard truth: if you're not comfortable with who you are, how are you going to feel comfortable around others?

Embrace Self-Love

Self-love is non-negotiable. It's what fuels you, especially when times get tough. Acknowledge the challenges you're facing instead of denying them because denial is a fast track to spiralling into negativity. It's also okay to admit you want friends and community—it's human. Set that as a goal and take action to achieve it.

Own Your Identity

Another critical part of self-love is embracing your identity. You are a unique combination of cultures, experiences, and values—own it! Recognize that your differences are strengths. In the story we explored earlier, the student learned to appreciate her mix of identities and used that as an advantage to connect with others. Drop the "this or that" mindset and don't pick one identity over another. When you fully embrace all parts of yourself, you can connect with people boldly, and the relationships you build will be meaningful because you're showing up as your authentic self.

Create a Value List

One crucial aspect of self-love is creating a value list. Ask yourself: What do I value in a friendship? What kind of friends do I need in my life? As an international student, it's tempting to try and be friends with everyone, but it's perfectly fine—even preferable—to have just one solid friend who ticks all your boxes. Quality over quantity, always. Present yourself authentically, and trust that the right people will be drawn to you. Don't settle out of fear or desperation and the right friendships will come when you stay true to yourself.

Ditch the Victim Mentality

Here's a tough pill to swallow: if you don't love yourself, others won't either. Sitting in self-pity won't magically attract the relationships you crave. You have to take a good look in the mirror and decide if building a support network is something you genuinely want and if it is, then move forward with that intention. Self-love is an action, not just a feeling.

Take the Initiative: Open Up and Put Yourself Out There

One of the most crucial steps in finding a community is opening up and putting yourself out there and I get it, putting yourself out there is terrifying. But here's the deal: no one is going to tap you on the shoulder and fix your loneliness for you. If you want community, you've got to make the first move. Humans are wired for connection—you're not meant to do life alone. Build your village and surround yourself with people who will have your back. This is a non-negotiable step for your well-being and success.

Leave the Past Behind

One of the most crucial tips I love to give international students when it comes to finding friends and community is to let go of the past to make room for the future. Many international students struggle to make friends because they are too homesick and refuse to leave their past lives and try to embrace new ones. No one wants to be friends with someone who keeps reminiscing about their past, like the friends they had and what they did. The reality is, those days are gone. It's time to focus on building your new life.

For most international students, the whole point of moving to another country was to build a better life. If you keep looking at what you left behind, how are you going to be able to create the life you want? You sacrificed so much, such as leaving your friends and family, so you owe it to yourself to be happy and hustle to build a network. Now, no one's saying you can't stay connected with your old friends and family, but don't let those relationships stop you from forming new ones. Trust the process. Leave the past behind, and permit yourself to step boldly into this new chapter.

Be Intentional

You have to learn to be intentional and excited about meeting new people. I remember speaking with a friend about this topic when I was preparing to write this book, and she shared her experience. When she was navigating university life, she deliberately chose to live in international student housing to experience different cultures and meet new people. She didn't sit around waiting for friendships to fall into her lap—she went out to common areas and started conversations. It's that level of intentionality that makes the difference.

Get Involved in Social Activities

Getting involved! Step out of your comfort zone and join clubs, associations, or groups that interest you. The student in our earlier story found her community through these activities. It doesn't always have to be university-related either. Religious events, book clubs, or even volunteer programs can connect you with like-minded people.

For example, my university usually hosts an orientation for new international students before the returning and domestic student orientation begins. I missed mine due to visa issues, and when I finally got to campus, I was amazed at how familiar some international students were with each other. Turns out, many of them met at that orientation, and because the activities encouraged collaboration, they quickly bonded. Hence, don't miss out on opportunities like these!

Avoid Prejudice and Overcome the Fear of Rejection

As an international student, successfully building friendships and a community requires avoiding prejudice. It's easy to let preconceived notions creep in, but these will only hold you back. Every culture has its own rules, and judging others by your standards is a sure way to miss out on meaningful connections.

Some international students tend to project their insecurities onto others, especially when they're worried about being rejected. It's a natural defence mechanism—if you expect someone to judge or dismiss you, you might act like they already have, even if they haven't. The problem with this is it creates a barrier before the other person even has a chance to show you who they are. To prevent this, present yourself authentically. Drop those preconceptions and stop assuming you know what others think of you. The truth is, you don't. Not until you give them—and yourself—a chance. When you meet someone, don't jump to conclusions about whether they'd make a good friend or not. For all you know, the person who seems distant or uninterested could be the kindest, most helpful person you'll ever meet. They might even be the connection that helps you level up in your personal, academic, or professional life. The world is full of surprises, and people are no different. If a conversation doesn't go the way you hoped, don't let it throw you off. Shake it off, say, "So what?" and keep moving forward. Fear of rejection is only as powerful as you allow it to be. Maintain a positive mentality, stay open, and trust that the right connections will come when you show up as your true self.

Overcome Ethnocentrism

Some international students fall into the trap of ethnocentrism without even realizing it. It's often rooted in fear—fear of rejection, fear of not fitting in, or just sticking with what feels comfortable. Ethnocentrism is the belief that you can only truly connect with people from your own ethnic or cultural group, and it leads to viewing the world through the narrow lens of your own culture's values and standards.

But here's the problem: when you let ethnocentrism take over, you're not only judging other cultures based on your own, but you might even develop a sense of superiority without meaning to. And that mindset can seriously limit your experience. You're not in your new country to recreate your old life—you're here to grow, learn, and expand your horizons. Sticking only to people who look, talk, and think like you will keep you in a bubble, and you'll miss out on all the amazing, diverse connections you could be making.

Embrace Diversity

As an international student, it's essential to stay open and curious— just be cautiously optimistic. Embracing diversity isn't about blindly jumping into every new experience; it's about recognizing that everyone has their own story, culture, and perspective. When you approach others with this mindset, you can build a more inclusive and supportive community, one that values each person's unique contribution.

Before I started university, I was convinced that only Nigerians could understand my humour, my culture, and my banter. I thought making friends with other races or ethnicities was out of the question. Oh, I was so wrong! To my surprise, I ended up in a diverse friend group with people from different races, ethnicities, and religions. What united us wasn't where we came from—it was our shared values, goals, and experiences. We were all international students with the same vision of creating a better life for ourselves in Canada and making our families proud. By accepting our cultural differences and embracing each other's strengths, we built strong, lasting connections.

Finding Your Support Network

There are people out there who are meant to be part of your support system in this new environment. But it won't just happen by magic. You have to put in the work—be proactive, push through the loneliness, and fight the fear of judgment. Building your support network takes time and effort, but by staying open-minded, overcoming ethnocentric habits, and embracing the diversity around you, you'll find genuine relationships that will enrich your life and help you thrive in your new world.

Chapter 5

Navigating Financial Challenges: From Survival to Stability

"Having a conversation with my parents about schooling in Canada felt like the most terrifying thing I had ever done. I raved about the countless opportunities awaiting me—like learning to drive without anyone constantly worrying about my safety and the limitless freedom and growth I could experience as a seventeen-year-old girl. I imagined all the daring adventures and eye-opening experiences that awaited me. In my mind, no obstacles and no barriers could hold me back. But my parents didn't share my excitement; they couldn't care less about my dreams. After endless discussions and countless tear-soaked pillowcases, they reluctantly agreed to support my decision to study in Canada. The realization that my dream life was finally within reach filled me with boundless joy.

In the blink of an eye, my visa and study permit were ready, and off I went to Canada with my mum by my side. Though I couldn't travel alone due to my age, I didn't mind—just setting foot in my promised land was all that mattered. The moment I landed, I sensed I was precisely where I was meant to be—Nigeria would always be my homeland, but Canada had become my new home. As days turned into weeks and then months, I gradually realized the extent of my sheltered upbringing. I had to learn the ropes of living in this new land and mastering everyday tasks on my own. After my first year, I started to get the hang of things, and even better, my parents were covering my tuition and accommodation fees, so there wasn't much to worry about. However, things took a horrible turn in my third year.

Unfortunately, my dad encountered some financial challenges, and my mum fell ill. Upon hearing the news, I felt like I was sinking into the ground. Tears welled up in my eyes as thoughts of an uncertain future flooded my mind. The life I had been living and still hoped to live now hung by a fragile thread. Where do I even begin, I wondered. I had grown up in such a sheltered home where everything was provided for me as if on a silver platter. This was my worst nightmare. For days, I cried, as each day served as a painful reminder of the uncertain future ahead, fraught with challenges and obstacles I had never imagined facing. I cried so much that I lacked the strength to think and carry out the next steps. After a few weeks of wailing and pushing the elephant in the room aside, I had to come to terms with my reality and concentrate on my goal and vision.

Failure wasn't an option for me. As the first member of my polygamous family to study abroad, I couldn't afford to falter. Since the beginning of my journey to Canada for school, my stepmother had vehemently opposed my decision and insisted on my failure.

Now, with my father facing financial difficulties and my mother's illness, I couldn't allow my stepmother's negative expectations to become reality. I needed to prove them wrong. I used their doubts as motivation to fuel my determination and knew I had to persevere and complete my studies, regardless of the obstacles. So, I sat down, asked myself some key questions, and began researching ways to earn money.

Coincidentally, this happened during the last semester of my third year, giving me the entire summer with 40-hour work weeks. After a few weeks, I secured a job as a server at a nearby pub. However, the wages didn't meet my needs, so I found another job at a popular supermarket in town. This arrangement seemed perfect at first, allowing me to work mornings at the store and nights at the pub. But as time went on, things became increasingly difficult. I found myself working non-stop for months on end, leaving home at 6 am and returning from the pub at midnight. Standing all day at work left my feet in agonizing pain. It was mentally, emotionally, and physically draining. There were moments when I wished to disappear from the world entirely. This wasn't the life I had envisioned or prayed for.

On top of it all, I had siblings to support at home since my parents couldn't fully provide for them. I was responsible for so many people and things that I had barely any money left for myself. With so many financial obligations, my paychecks disappeared quickly, leaving me with just enough to cover rent and groceries and nothing left for savings. Things grew worse when it began to affect my academics. I could barely enroll in courses of my choice because of the delay in tuition payment on my account. I would find myself constantly rearranging my course schedule to obtain my degree based on priority so I could at least catch a class needed to get my degree. After constant back and forth, I started to grow tired of these challenges. I had to do something about my finances and navigate the intricacies of this currency.

I started to research more about how to save money as a student and invest my money. I learned to analyze my spending habits through my bank's mobile apps, build a budget, and cut unnecessary expenses. I became highly frugal with my money and found ways to gain student discounts on everything I bought. I also researched several resources like scholarships and bursaries to fund my tuition and some of my expenses. I knew I had to do everything that I possibly could to succeed, even if it meant working two jobs, avoiding every temptation to overspend, or looking for every coupon I possibly could. I began to delve deep into the intricacies of investing in various capitals, including stocks and buying properties.

The following school year, I became quite proactive in searching for ways to add value, enhance my skill sets, and secure a stable corporate job. While holding those two jobs, I started volunteering in the corporate space as I was pursuing a minor in business management. I also started to network and engage on social platforms to gain exposure to employers, external scholarships and fundraisers. A couple of months later, I was able to get a steady job. However, I quickly realized I needed to learn how to negotiate if I wanted the pay I was aiming for, given my circumstances. I realized that if I didn't ask for what I wanted, it would never be given to me. The more I asked and knew, the more leverage I got. I eventually secured the pay I desired, which allowed me to manage my financial burdens. Gradually, my finances started to stabilize, and I finally felt like I could breathe again."

A girl from Lagos, Nigeria.

Financial challenges are one of the biggest hurdles international students face today. And let's be real—it can be downright agonizing. Studying abroad isn't for the faint of heart. You're not just dealing with high tuition fees; there are living expenses, currency fluctuations, and a whole list of other costs that domestic students don't have to think about as much. While domestic students may have access to financial aid, scholarships, and affordable housing, international students often have limited options. And to make matters worse, your immigration status usually limits your work opportunities, making financial stability even harder to achieve.

The Harsh Reality of Limited Support

As the storyteller described, this situation can feel particularly brutal, especially when there's a lack of direct support. Many international students are forced to "scavenge" for resources in a new environment and the harsh reality is that a lot of international students, whether self-sponsored or not, don't have financial safety nets. There's no guarantee that they, their families, or guardians will have the financial means to support them through their entire academic journey. Living with that kind of uncertainty can be terrifying. It's like a soldier being deployed and knowing that there's no promise of a safe return or everything being intact when they get back. It's a risk, but it's one we all take.

The Many Faces of Financial Strain

These financial struggles come in varying degrees. Maybe you're just scraping by to cover your living expenses, or maybe you're in a full- blown crisis trying to pay your tuition fees. Either way, the impact is real, and it can derail your entire academic journey. I've seen students who couldn't enrol in their classes because they couldn't pay tuition, which delayed their graduation and threw their entire academic plan off track. When money issues consume your thoughts, it's hard to focus on anything else—studies, social life, or even your future. It's a vicious cycle: you stress about money, your grades slip, and then you stress even more because now you're behind academically.

The Mental Health Toll

Financial stress doesn't just affect your academics—it weighs heavily on your mental health. The constant worry about how to survive financially can cause serious anxiety and leave you feeling mentally and emotionally overwhelmed. It's hard to stay focused on your goals when your brain is consumed with worry. That's why it's essential to develop a strategy and the right mindset—one that helps you overcome these financial obstacles. It's not easy, but it's possible. Millions of international students faced these same struggles and made it through. And guess what? You can too!

OVERCOMING FINANCIAL CHALLENGES

Create and establish financial safety nets

Let's talk about something serious—financial safety nets. Many international students don't have them, and trust me, it's a risky game to play. One of the biggest mistakes I see is students not planning ahead, especially when it comes to their finances. As an international student, you have to be proactive. That means sitting down with your guardians, family, or anyone who's helping fund your education, and having a real conversation about alternative financial options. What happens if things go sideways? What's the backup plan? Ask further questions like: Do I have a trust fund or money saved up somewhere that I can access? Do you have life insurance? Don't just assume that your parents or guardians have you covered; ask for evidence! Think about the student in our story—she could have explored different ways to fund her education and living expenses if something happened to her parents. It's not about being pessimistic; it's about being prepared. The last thing you want is to find yourself stranded financially, especially when you've got enough on your plate already as an international student.

Secure a Mentor and Guardian

One smart move you can make as an international student is to secure a mentor or guardian in your study country—someone who can act as a financial guarantor or a go-to person during emergencies. Let me give you a personal example. When I arrived in Canada, my parents arranged for trusted friends to serve as my "surrogate parents." These guardians were my lifeline, especially during emergencies, whether financial or health-related. During the COVID pandemic, for instance, when my parents were hesitant to cover university accommodation costs due to rising expenses, I was fortunate to stay with my guardians for the school year. No worries about rent or food—it was a huge relief! The key takeaway here is to establish a solid relationship with someone outside your immediate family who's in your country of study. They can step in when unexpected challenges arise, particularly financial ones.

Explore University Scholarships and Bursaries

Don't sleep on university scholarships and bursaries. Many institutions offer scholarships to international students right from the get-go, but there are tons more if you put in the effort to apply. Maintaining a solid academic standing can also open doors to multiple scholarships per year. While some scholarships may seem limited to citizens of certain countries, international students may still qualify due to low applicant numbers. Some students have even built relationships with professors and deans, which not only provided guidance but also led to other funding opportunities. The bottom line is–ask questions, forge connections, and explore all the available resources. There's more support out there than you might think—grab it!

Understand the basics of how to manage your finances

Many international students dive into their new lives without understanding the financial landscape of their study destination, and it often leads to irresponsible spending or, oddly enough, excessive saving. Waiting until financial issues hit before you learn to budget and spend wisely is like jumping into the deep end without knowing how to swim. It's not the smartest move. From day one, familiarize yourself with the local financial system. How do people spend money in your new country? Are cash transactions common, or is everyone swiping cards? Take Canada, for example—credit card usage is huge here, and if you're not careful, failing to track your credit card payments can pile up debt faster than you think. Learn the cost of living, inflation rates, and general expenses–a simple trick could be to compare the price of basic items like groceries, say the cost of apples, over a few months to see how prices shift.

Create a Budget

Now that you have a grip on how money works in your new environment, it's time to create a budget. Outline all your essential expenses— rent, groceries, subscriptions, and bills and seek input from trusted locals or fellow students to gauge average costs in your area. Over time, as you become more comfortable with your surroundings and preferences, your spending patterns will become clearer and you can tailor your budget accordingly. Also, many banking apps now make budgeting easier by offering features that track your spending and allocate budgets. As your life evolves—whether you land a job or experience changes in living costs—adjust your budget to align with your current goals and financial priorities.

Avoid an Extravagant Lifestyle

Lastly, resist the temptation to keep up with the Johnsons-extravagant lifestyles. It's super tempting to want to keep up with everyone else's lifestyle, especially in university where social activities and appearances are everything. But let me give it to you straight—spending outside your means is a fast track to financial stress. Don't fall into the trap of peer pressure. Just because everyone's out grabbing wings or bubble tea doesn't mean you need to join every single time. If you can't afford it, don't sweat it—say no and move on. If sticking to your budget becomes tough, get an accountability partner. This could be a mentor or someone you trust, who can help you check in on your spending habits and keep you on track. Make it a habit to schedule regular check-ins to see where you can improve. Trust me, developing these habits now will save you a lot of stress and give you the financial discipline to face any unexpected challenges head-on.

Desire and learn to add value

In most societies, your value is directly tied to the impact you make. And, if you think about it, money often comes in exchange for that value. Look around you—whether it's in your classes, school clubs, or even within your friend group—there are endless opportunities to add value and solve problems. The moment you step into a new environment, no matter how tight or thick your finances may be, seek ways to contribute and add value. In the Western world, domestic students are raised with the mindset of always adding value, which makes financial negotiations a lot easier for them. It's second nature. As an international student, cultivating this same habit will not only position you for financial gain but also help you reach your financial goals more quickly. The key is to constantly seek opportunities to contribute, this could be as simple as volunteering, getting a part-time job, or becoming active in your school's clubs. Once you make yourself valuable, you'll find that financial opportunities start to open up, and bargaining becomes much more accessible.

Job Hunting and Networking

When it comes to job hunting, don't wait until your last penny is gone before you start looking. As an international student, the earlier you get your networking hat on, the better. Seek out job opportunities, even if they're small or part-time. Besides the obvious career benefits, working allows you to build a solid savings cushion for when things get rough. And trust me, that emergency fund can be a real lifesaver when you're hit with unexpected financial challenges. Take the example from the story earlier: the student didn't waste time finding jobs to help ease her parents' financial burden. Even if your family can cover your expenses, having your savings gives you independence. Plus, getting a job early helps you learn how the financial system works in your new country. Over time, earning your own money not only feels great but also helps you build capital and financial responsibility.

The Power of Negotiation

When you bring value to the table, it gives you leverage, and leverage gives you power to negotiate. Most people associate negotiating with job offers, but it often goes deeper than that. Sometimes you don't even know what you can get until you ask. Whether it's for better pay, leveraging valuable information, or improving your situation, negotiation is a skill you need to master. For example, in the story we talked about earlier, the student didn't just accept the first offer—she negotiated and increased her pay. As an international student, don't settle for less, whether it's for a job, resources, or assistance. However, to negotiate effectively, you need to back it up with confidence and a solid understanding of what you bring to the table. The more value you add, the more recognized you become, and the more empowered you'll feel when negotiating. Knowledge is power, and with the right information, you can turn that power into money and opportunities.

Establish a "this too shall surely pass!" mindset

I get it—facing financial challenges as an international student can feel like swallowing a bitter pill. But here's the reality: you will get through it. Don't run away from the challenge or ignore it, hoping it will disappear. The fact that it's knocking on your door means you have what it takes to face it head-on and conquer it. And yes, I know you've probably heard this a thousand times throughout this book (and probably from every motivational speaker ever), but challenges are the building blocks of success. The key to overcoming them is to keep your focus on the bigger picture—your vision. Every challenge you face will shape you, prune you, and prepare you—mentally, physically, and emotionally—for what's ahead.

Remember the student in the story we discussed earlier? She's now a renowned manager leading one of the major ministries within the Government of Alberta. She's written books on financial management and even runs her own consulting business. Her challenges didn't defeat her—they revealed her passion for helping others manage their finances. Now, your story might not unfold exactly like hers, but trust me, the lessons you're learning now will serve you and others well in the future. Take note of those lessons, because they'll help you grow, thrive, and impact those around you.

Also, don't ever be ashamed of your current financial situation. Embrace it. It's a season, not your final destination. Don't beat yourself up because you're working extra jobs to make ends meet, and don't compare yourself to others who may seem to have it easier. This period of hard work is temporary. You're putting in the effort now because you know it's going to pay off down the road. So, keep this in mind: challenges are the foundation for your future success. Keep pushing forward, and you'll come out stronger on the other side.

Chapter 6

The Art of Networking: Building Connections and Creating Opportunities

"I was just in 10th grade when I decided to study in Canada for university. Out of curiosity, I began to research universities in Canada. I encountered countless videos about the Rocky Mountains and Banff within the City of Calgary, and soon enough the University of Calgary caught my attention. I wanted to study in a place with lots of mountains and expansive landscapes, where I could experience adventures to tell my children when I was older. After I had done more research, I emailed about ten different universities, including the University of Calgary, to learn more about their admission processes.

As I reached grade 12, I decided to start my university application process with my parents. Unfortunately, they weren't too fond of my interest in the University of Calgary and wanted me to study in Ontario because my older brothers had completed their undergraduate degrees there. They raved about the endless opportunities and the vibrant life in Toronto, however, my mind was still fixed on the University of Calgary. Submerged by the growing pressure from my family, I agreed to apply to universities in Ontario. Finally, I received an offer from Wilfrid Laurier University and began enrolling in courses. I never felt so irritated in my life. One would expect I should be extremely happy about the offer but I was distraught–realising I had lost the chance to attend my dream university.

After much contemplation, I decided to take matters into my own hands. At the last minute and without telling anyone, I applied to the University of Calgary and received an offer letter quickly. Immediately, I dropped all my courses at Wilfrid Laurier and enrolled in some courses at the University of Calgary. When my family heard about the switch, they were furious "furious" is an understatement. They thought my decision was irrational and uncalculated. They were also displeased with my choice of a Business program, preferring traditional fields like engineering, medicine, or law. Despite their disapproval, I knew I wouldn't enjoy those programs and was a "business guy" at heart. After much back and forth with my family, I decided to study the program of my choice without their financial aid.

You might wonder, "Is this guy crazy? That's thousands of dollars to be paid every year as tuition." I had a vision of the life I wanted to build and was willing to do anything to get there. I couldn't live my life making others happy or meeting their expectations while neglecting my dreams. I also had a big goal of starting a start-up right after finishing my studies, and I realized I needed to start working towards kickstarting my career as soon as possible.

A WORD FOR AN INTERNATIONAL STUDENT

Once I landed in Canada, I knew I had to secure a stable, well-paying job immediately. I had no Canadian experience and was unsure where to start, but I understood my end goal and didn't care if I had to sacrifice sleep or my social life to achieve it. I applied for some menial jobs and began working two jobs simultaneously. While these positions allowed me to pay off some tuition, I realized it wasn't sustainable. I needed well-paying jobs to fulfill my goal, so I started networking.

First, I had to determine what field I was interested in to start my career. I created a LinkedIn account and grew my contacts, understanding that forming connections with people in my area of interest and beyond was crucial to getting a good job quickly. However, I realized I didn't know how to network professionally. Questions flooded my mind: 'How do I introduce myself?', 'What do I say?'. These questions ignited a fear that I wouldn't be able to attain my goal as fast as I wanted. After much internal debate and encouragement from friends, I decided to attend my first networking event.

As I arrived at the event, I realized I had no strategy. Overwhelming questions filled my mind, and anxiety made me sick to my stomach. "What have I gotten myself into?" I asked myself. At that moment, I remembered my goal and vision and the anxiety subsided, and I devised a plan. I quickly outlined a summary of who I was and my background, wrote down questions I was curious about, and set a goal to talk to at least five people and establish a connection with three of the five people I met.

As I walked around, I encountered many CEOs of start-ups and big corporate companies. I walked up to a few of them and began sharing my story, the skills I had gained, and the skills I wanted to develop. Surprisingly, my story resonated with them. As I got along with more people, my confidence grew, and I stayed at the event for a few more hours. I was curious about how these individuals became so successful and wanted to learn about their productivity habits and career hacks. I asked many questions like, "What brings you here? What do you do? What advice would you give to your younger self? I am somewhat new to Calgary—what do you do for fun here?". After the event, I requested contact information from the people I spoke with and followed up for coffee meetings.

After establishing and sustaining a relationship with one of the people I met, I was offered my first corporate job. I quickly realized the importance of building relationships with people in my field. Networking became a wonderful strategy to achieve my goals while meeting brilliant individuals. I continued networking and found unconventional and non-traditional ways to connect and make myself memorable. I remember sneaking into an event for students from a specific university, even though I wasn't a student there. Despite my nerves, I had a wonderful conversation with the co-founder of a prominent start-up company at the event.

I shared my story and learned about the co-founder and the company. We kept in touch, and I expressed my desire to help in various aspects of the business. Although they couldn't pay me, I didn't mind working for free to gain specific skills and work experience. While working with them, I met four amazing people—

two are now good friends, and two are mentors who run a program at a university outside Calgary. Through this relationship, I received resources and implemented ideas to improve the program. I grew to love networking, attending more events, and finding creative ways to connect with people. Sometimes, I would purposely leave my jacket at networking events to have a reason to return and network further.

My quest to fulfill my vision and goal ignited a love for meeting and networking with people. I realized that establishing a mindset and love for creating and building relationships makes the art of networking quite easy."

A boy from Gujarat, India.

Networking is the art of sharing or exchanging ideas and information with people, whether in formal or informal settings. It's about building relationships with those you've never met, finding common interests, and creating opportunities that benefit both parties. As an international student, it can feel overwhelming to find resources, a support system, or even a job when you first land in a new country. This is exactly where networking steps in. It's a tool that, when used effectively, can help you form relationships, access resources, and even kickstart your career. However, it must be done with the right mindset and approach.

Why is Networking Called an Art?

Networking is called an art because, like any art, it requires skill and a bit of finesse. You have to think about things like your overall goal, shared interests, body language, timing, and, of course, your value proposition. Every time you meet someone, you're making an impression, so you need a strategy to ensure it's a positive one. Networking can take many shapes–from social media platforms like LinkedIn to attending in-person events or having a casual conversation at Starbucks—it's all networking. The key is recognizing that every interaction is a potential opportunity. The fact that it requires some level of strategy doesn't mean you should be scared. Many international students shy away from networking, thinking it's full of pressure or that they don't have enough to offer. Let's put that myth to rest: Networking takes practice, and the more you do it, the better you become.

Misconceptions About Networking

Networking is "Only" for Job Hunting

One of the biggest misconceptions international students have about networking is that it's only necessary when you're looking for a job. Let me be clear: this mindset is holding you back–it's hindering your success and creating unnecessary pressure. Networking is so much more than job hunting—it's about sharing information, exchanging ideas, and building relationships based on mutual interests. Although job opportunities come from networking, they're often a byproduct of the meaningful connections you create, not the sole purpose. As an international student, you need to start networking the moment you arrive in your new country. Don't wait until your final year or when you're in a pinch to land a job or internship. Trust me, that's the worst time to start—I made that mistake. I waited until my third year, and when I finally started networking, it was obvious to everyone I was just there to find a job. The pressure was intense, and I felt like I was constantly "on the hunt." If I had started networking earlier—during my first or second year, when job pressure wasn't so high—I could have spent time building genuine relationships instead of desperately scrambling for leads.

When you focus on networking early, you're able to get to know people without the looming pressure of needing something from them. You're building relationships, and that's where the magic happens. Sometimes, the value of these connections isn't immediate, but it will pay off in the long run. A friend once told me how people have even met their life partners by networking at events! That's right—networking isn't just for professional relationships; it can lead to personal connections, too. The key is not to approach networking with a "give me" attitude. You never want to reach a point of desperation or entitlement. Instead, embrace the mindset of learning, growing, and contributing. Be humble— acknowledge that you're still new to this environment, and focus on building relationships that will last.

Networking is "Only" for Extroverts

Networking is not reserved exclusively for extroverts. As an international student, it can feel overwhelming, especially if you're unfamiliar with local communication norms. But here's the thing: networking isn't about being the loudest person in the room. You don't have to be an extrovert to connect with people effectively. All you need is the ability to express your interests among like-minded individuals. Whether it's in your professional field, with your classmates, or even in a shared hobby group, you already have the tools to network. Think about it—if you've ever worked on a group project, what did you do? You gravitated toward people in your class who seemed interesting or capable, right? That's networking! Maybe you've joined class groups on platforms like Discord or Facebook. That's networking too. You don't need to be the life of the party; you just need to know your interests and learn how to express them. Whatever you present with confidence will naturally appear more attractive to others.

People are Naturally Good at Networking

Another big misconception is that people are just magically good at networking right from the start. Wrong! Networking takes practice. Remember when you were a baby learning to walk? You didn't get it on the first try. You had to stand, wobble, and sometimes fall before you could stride confidently. Networking is the same. It takes time to master the art of juggling conversations, knowing when to chime in and when to hold back. Don't be hard on yourself. Just like anything else, practice makes progress. You're allowed to make mistakes and learn as you go. It's all part of the process.

Networking is confined to Professional Settings

Networking is not confined to only professional environments. In reality, networking can happen anywhere and at any time. Your classroom, community events, student gatherings, and even religious functions are all ripe opportunities for building connections. It doesn't always have to be in a formal setting; the key is to connect with people who may share diverse interests, locate similarities and be open to building relationships. While networking doesn't necessarily have to happen at professional events, these settings often provide opportunities to meet individuals with similar career aspirations. Simultaneously, you can use informal gatherings to hone your networking skills, allowing you to thrive in any environment. The goal is to be open to building relationships, regardless of the setting. Every interaction is a chance to connect, and who knows? That casual chat at a weekend event might just lead to the connection that propels you closer to your career goals.

Networking can seem daunting, maybe even a little intimidating, but the truth is it's a critical skill for building relationships and growing your career. People will get to know you through networking, and that's how they assess if you're the right fit for future collaborations or opportunities—and vice versa. Don't wait until the last minute. Start learning and practicing your networking skills from the moment you land in a new country. The sooner you start, the better you'll become at it.

OVERCOMING NETWORKING CHALLENGES

Get Comfortable with the Uncomfortable

Being an international student means stepping into unfamiliar territory, and you'll quickly find yourself in situations that might make you squirm. Success often comes from getting comfortable with the uncomfortable, and networking is no exception. Networking is all about engagement—connecting with people from different backgrounds, races, careers, and interests. It can feel intimidating at first, but trust me, anyone can do it! The key is finding ways to put yourself in environments where you can meet and interact with others. As an international student, your goal is to meet as many people as possible and to be socially present. Get a few friends together, compile a list of networking events, job fairs, or workshops at your school or in your city, and schedule dates to attend. You could also join online forums or meet-up groups to expand your reach. When you do show up, don't just stand in the corner. Ask questions, share your thoughts, and engage. Not only will this help you sharpen your networking skills, but you'll also start to feel more comfortable in these settings.

Volunteering to Build Skills and Relationships

One of the best ways to build your network and grow your skills simultaneously is through volunteering. In the Western world, volunteering is a major avenue for meeting people, gaining experience, and contributing to the community. The opportunities are endless—university clubs, faculty, food banks, local clinics, and community events are all great places to start. When you volunteer, you're putting yourself out there, meeting new people, building your skill set, and learning about your new environment. Take the story earlier, where the student chose to volunteer at a start-up. It opened doors for him to meet people, create relationships, and acquire new skills. A friend of mine had a similar experience. She started volunteering as a peer supporter at her university and got involved in student governance from her second year until she graduated. Initially, she did it because she enjoyed it, but little did she know that this passion project was building valuable skills. Over time, she developed solid customer service skills and gained a lot of confidence. Eventually, an employer noticed her dedication and interpersonal skills through her volunteer work and she got hired.

Leverage Social Media for Networking

Another effective way for international students to gain exposure is by establishing and maintaining a presence on social media platforms, particularly LinkedIn. Too many international students overlook social media's potential for networking until they're frantically searching for a job. Even worse, some create a profile but don't engage or showcase their skills. Create a LinkedIn profile early or as soon as you can and don't just slap on a few details and call it a day—be intentional. Highlight your skills, experiences, and professional activities. Give people a glimpse into who you are and what you bring to the table by sharing your interests and passions. Once your profile is up, connect with as many relevant people as possible. Seek out professionals in your field, fellow students, and alumni. And don't just passively scroll through your feed—engage! If you attended a cool conference or completed an exciting project, share it. Follow companies you want to work for, engage with recruiters, comment on posts, and send direct messages when appropriate. The more active you are, the more visible you become. This proactive approach could lead to internships, mentorships, or even job opportunities. Plenty of international students (and locals) have landed great opportunities just by being active on LinkedIn and other professional platforms.

Learn to Sell Yourself and Communicate Confidently

As an international student, you have to learn how to sell yourself and communicate effectively. A few weeks before I started writing this book, a friend hit me with a truth bomb: "In the Western world, talking is how you win, not working hard." It sounds harsh, but it's true. Here, networking and getting yourself in front of the right people and opportunities are all about how you present yourself—your ideas, personality, and story—through communication. Many of us come from cultures where hard work is the ultimate measure of success. While that's not entirely wrong, it's not the full picture in this part of the world. You'll quickly realize that it's not always the hardest worker who gets ahead; it's the most engaged, the one who can sell their story and ideas effectively.

While preparing to write this book, I went on a work date with a friend. During our time, I observed one of her colleagues during their team stand-up meeting. He was fully engaged, making sure to acknowledge everyone's opinions, even his manager's. I turned to my friend and said, "That guy is definitely getting promoted." Here, they say "work smart," not "work hard." Expressing yourself and highlighting your wins out loud is how you get noticed. The people who stand out and are remembered aren't necessarily the ones working behind the scenes— they're the ones sharing their wins, communicating their value, and telling compelling stories. These are the people who are voted for promotion, the most valued, or the desirable candidate to hire.

You have to learn how to express yourself and your wins verbally. Those who are most memorable often have the most compelling stories and can express themselves and their value well. For example, in the story you read earlier, the individual made an effort to share his story and engage with others, which made him quite memorable. The truth is, that not everyone is born with stellar speaking skills, but is can be developed. Look for opportunities to speak—discuss what you've learned in class, talk about your projects in your school clubs, or share insights from articles you've read. Although hard work can open doors, combining hard work with effective communication can open all doors. There are plenty of people working hard but not everyone is communicating effectively. So, if you want to get ahead, step out of your comfort zone, and start talking.

Build Your Brand

You might think it's too early in your career or university years to start thinking about branding, but it's never too early to consider your personal brand. Many international students, and even students in general, mistakenly believe that branding is only relevant for companies and entrepreneurs. This couldn't be further from the truth! As a growing professional, you need to start crafting your brand now. What do you want people to know you for? What makes you unique? When you think of Bill Gates or Elon Musk, certain things immediately come to mind—wealth, technological innovation, philanthropy, and so on.

Recently, a mentor asked a group of peers and me a thought-provoking question: "Do you want to be a thermostat or a thermometer?" A thermostat regulates the temperature of a room, while a thermometer simply tells you what the temperature is. When you walk into a networking event or a room full of people, do you want to set the tone and bring your unique personality—your brand—into the space, or do you just want to conform to the energy already there?

Stand Out

In a university setting, countless students are attending networking events or job fairs just like you. But what makes you stand out? What differentiates you from the masses of students that employers and professionals meet every day? Maybe it's the educational YouTube channel you started and grew to 100,000 subscribers within four years. Or perhaps it's the technology you developed as part of the robotics club that led to a groundbreaking achievement at your university. As an international student in a new environment, consider what you want to represent—the skills and qualifications, both professional (academic) and non-professional, that define you.

Building Your Brand Takes Time

Building your personal brand isn't something that happens overnight. It requires time, dedication, and a deep understanding of who you are and what you want to achieve. Many of your distinguishing qualities won't reveal themselves until you explore and find ways to awaken your talents and interests. That's why building your brand takes time. Start small, like within your classroom or a team project. You might become known as the funny person in your group, or the one who's always punctual. As you gain confidence, this could evolve into being recognized for your presentation skills or expertise in a particular subject. As you grow, you'll become more comfortable showcasing your brand, which will naturally carry over into your professional life.

Your brand is not just about what you do but also about how you present yourself and how others perceive you. The sooner you start thinking about and developing your brand, the more you'll stand out in your field, and the more opportunities you'll attract. Remember, your brand is an evolving reflection of your growth, skills, and personality—so embrace the journey of building it with confidence.

Master the Art

Networking is an art that requires a clear goal and a well-crafted strategy. As an international student, you already bring a wealth of skills, experiences, and stories with you. The key is to take the time to present these attributes in a way that leaves a lasting impression. But remember—networking isn't just about selling yourself. It's about creating a meaningful exchange, where both parties feel seen, heard, and understood.

Set Goals for Networking

First things first—set goals. Networking without a plan is like wandering around a new city without a map. Setting clear goals keeps you focused and accountable, making it easier to achieve your desired outcomes. For example, the individual in the story earlier set a goal for his first networking event: speak with five people and connect with at least three who shared similar interests. These small goals help take the pressure off and make networking more manageable.

You can also turn goal-setting into a fun activity like a game. If you attend a networking event with friends, you might compete to see who can meet the most people or gather the most contacts, and maybe throw in a prize for the winner. Alternatively, you can set personal goals, like learning three new things about the people you meet—whether it's about their career or something as random as their pet's name. The key is to make sure your goals align with what you want to achieve. Additionally, avoid setting unrealistic or trivial goals, it will only lead to frustration and inefficiency.

Create a Networking Strategy

Once you have your goals in place, the next step is to develop a strategy. As you grow in your journey as an international student, it's essential to know your career interests, skills, and what steps to take during and after networking, especially in professional settings.

Start by perfecting your elevator pitch—a short and concise introduction that highlights your professional achievements and skills. This pitch should include your area of study, any relevant skills you've gained, and your career aspirations. Be clear about what you're studying, the relevant skills you've developed, and your career aspirations. For instance, if you're studying software engineering, talk about your educational background, technical skills and achievements. But don't just list out qualifications like a robot; deliver your pitch with enthusiasm. In the Western world, how you communicate says as much about you as what you say. Enthusiasm shows you're confident, teachable, and engaged.

Ask Meaningful and Engaging Questions

Networking isn't just about what you say—it's also about the questions you ask. Prepare a list of questions ahead of time to show you're genuinely interested–I call it the "cheat sheet"; and if you have done some research about the event you are networking at, even better. Try not to jump straight to typical questions like "What do you do?" Get creative. Ask questions that will make you memorable. For example, the individual in the story asked a mix of light-hearted and serious questions that left a positive impression. If you're nervous, start with an ice-breaker question like, "I'm new to the area—what do you do for fun around here?" or "That jacket is awesome! Where'd you get it?" These openers are easy and put the other person at ease. As the conversation flows, dive deeper with questions like, "What projects are you currently working on?" or "How did you get started in this field?" Show that you're actively listening by finding ways to relate to their experiences. And don't be afraid to ask for advice. For example, "I'm interested in entering that field. Maybe we could connect, and I could learn more from you."

Also, social etiquette matters. Always gauge the comfort level of the person you're speaking with. For example, complimenting someone's perfume might be fine if you're talking from woman to woman, but could be misinterpreted if directed at a man. It's all about reading the room and being respectful.

Follow Up After Networking

After making a connection, the next step is to follow up. Think of it like going on a date—if you enjoyed the conversation, you or the other person is likely to reach out the next day. Send a quick follow-up email or LinkedIn message. Thank them for their time and mention specific topics you discussed to show you were paying attention. If they gave you advice, express your gratitude and maybe mention how you're already applying it. Don't be shy about suggesting a follow-up meeting or a casual coffee chat to keep the conversation going. Taking the initiative will leave a lasting impression and improve your chances of being remembered for future opportunities.

Do Not Overthink the Process

Many international students often feel anxious about networking, worrying whether they'll be relatable or liked. Here's the thing: adopt a "so what" attitude! A wise person once told me, "If you're scared of a particular outcome—like not making the right impression or lacking confidence—just ask yourself, 'So what? What's the worst that could happen?'" Nine times out of ten, putting genuine effort into conversations and relationships leads to positive results. Overthinking often leads to negative outcomes, so take a step back and breathe. It can make a smooth interaction into a stressful mess. The person you're talking to is human too, probably dealing with their anxieties. Learn to stay relaxed and positive, and engage in small talk to ease tension.

Networking is a key professional and social tool, especially when you're new to a place. The earlier you start, the better. Even if you're still learning the ins and outs, beginning early helps you get comfortable faster and allows you to build relationships sooner, giving you a head start in your career. Remember this: you already have the capability, the skills, and the confidence to network—it just takes that little push to step out of your comfort zone. By embracing the "so what" mindset and focusing on making genuine connections, you'll see that networking becomes less intimidating and more rewarding over time. Stop stressing about it and start enjoying the process!

Chapter 7

Breaking Free from Comparison: Building Confidence

"I arrived in Canada at the age of sixteen, and unlike most students, I wasn't filled with excitement. Instead, I was terrified of the uncertainty that lay ahead. I felt unprepared for the responsibilities and independence that awaited me. Back home in Nigeria, I had never had to manage anything on my own— my finances, my schedule etc–everything was done for me. My life had been straightforward, with clear expectations set by my family. There was never a need for me to stand up for myself, express my emotions, or show any form of grit. But in Canada, everything changed. I had to decide when to go to bed, how to manage my time, how to manage my finances and navigate a completely different educational system. This newfound freedom and autonomy were both exciting and overwhelming. I quickly realized that I had to work hard and smart to get what I wanted as my sheltered background had not prepared me for this.

As I began my university journey, I noticed how bold and articulate many of my domestic peers were. They joined bands, participated in clubs, and took on various projects to facilitate their personal and professional growth. As time went on, their confidence and activity levels began to bother me because I felt underutilized and inexperienced. Stories of students starting companies or engaging in passion projects that turned into significant successes made me feel even more inadequate. "Would I ever be as good as them?" I constantly wondered. My conclusion always led to the belief that, as an international student, I was at a disadvantage in society—essentially, I couldn't excel as others did. While others explored new opportunities, I often found myself curling into a ball, overwhelmed by my insecurities. These constant thoughts kept eating away at me, and I never felt good enough for anything. Over time, my confidence began to diminish.

This constant fear and low self-esteem persisted throughout my university journey to the point where I would cry for days on end. During one of my classes in my third year, we were asked to give a presentation as part of our assignment. Being the diligent student that I was, I prepared and practiced extensively. On the day of the presentation, I was excited to give it my all. However, as soon as my name was called, I began to sweat profusely, and a sudden surge of fear and anxiety overwhelmed me. As I stood in front of the class, my mind raced with doubts: "Would I fumble? Would they understand what I was saying? Is what I'm saying smart enough?" These thoughts plagued me as I nervously delivered my presentation. When it ended, the silence in the room was deafening. Thoughts raced through my mind: "Did I fumble? Was there something wrong with my pronunciation?" Unbeknownst to me, during the entire presentation, my notes were visible on the screen due to a technical error I wasn't aware of. When I finally realized this, I was mortified. I was ready to go six feet under. The air felt tighter, and I could hear my heart racing as I struggled to hold back tears. I immediately ran to my dorm and cried hopelessly, feeling utterly defeated.

Gradually, my lack of confidence began to extend beyond the classroom. I started avoiding networking events because I didn't know my value proposition or what to say. I was fixated on perfection and believed I had no experience worth sharing. After classes, I would isolate myself in my room, napping or studying alone, while others worked part-time jobs and socialized. Comparing myself to others, I constantly felt I wasn't speaking as well, performing as well academically, or connecting with others as much. This constant comparison fostered a deep-seated belief that I had nothing valuable to offer. My mind was preoccupied with thoughts of inadequacy, leading to a persistent sense of imposter syndrome and a lack of confidence. I often felt like an outsider, too afraid to speak up in class or participate in discussions, worried about what others might think of me.

Eventually, I grew tired of feeling inferior and decided to take action. I took some time to reflect on my journey as an international student and listed all my accomplishments and the things I was good at, focusing on my strengths rather than my perceived weaknesses. Upon reflection, I realized that the decision to move to a new country as a teenager was itself an accomplishment—a bold move that not many people could take. I recognized that I was actually at an advantage because I had the opportunity to learn a new culture while retaining my own, making my multifaceted identity more relatable and helping me connect with diverse people on multiple levels. I created an affirmations list and began affirming myself daily. I also started meditating and visualizing myself doing activities I was too afraid to do at the time, like participating in classroom interactions, networking, or engaging in social gatherings. Through these affirmations and visualization, my confidence slowly began to grow again.

After university, I was fortunate to find a mentor who offered guidance and support. These mentorship sessions were transformative. They provided a safe space for me to express my fears and receive constructive feedback. Through these interactions, I learned to articulate my value proposition and gained the confidence to attend networking events. I also got involved in activities where I excelled, allowing me to showcase my skills and build my self-esteem.

Slowly but surely, my confidence grew. Thoughts of inadequacy were silenced and thoughts of reassurement began to rise. I learned to stop comparing myself to others and started celebrating my unique journey, achievements and skills. I could confidently speak about the value I brought and what made me unique. By focusing on my strengths and actively seeking growth opportunities, I overcame my imposter syndrome and built a stronger sense of self-worth."

A girl from Port Harcourt, Nigeria.

Many international students struggle with confidence when they move abroad, often finding themselves caught in the comparison trap— measuring their abilities and achievements against those of their peers. In a new environment, where the standards of excellence are unfamiliar, it's easy to feel the urge to constantly compare your progress with that of locals. This often leads to feelings of inferiority and inadequacy. Watching others thrive while you struggle can make you doubt your abilities and accomplishments, and that doubt can quickly spiral into low self-esteem.

The Comparison Trap

This cycle of comparison and low self-esteem can affect nearly every aspect of an international student's life: academics, social relationships, career prospects, and even networking efforts. A lot of this doubt stems from the assumption that local students are inherently more competent or better adapted to the environment—an illusion, in most cases. Many international students automatically see themselves as beginners, subconsciously placing themselves in an inferior position and hesitating to engage fully with their new surroundings.

Previous Experience and Preparedness

Confidence issues can also arise from a lack of experience or preparedness. As an international student, you may have come from a background where you weren't required to be as independent or to face challenges on your own—similar to what the student experienced in the story you read earlier. Moving abroad can thrust you into situations that demand self-reliance and problem-solving skills that you may not be used to yet. The realization that this level of independence is the baseline expectation in your new environment can feel overwhelming and frustrating, especially when it seems like your local peers are navigating it with ease.

Pressure to Succeed

Another factor that can fuel the comparison trap is the intense pressure to succeed. International students often face significant pressure to excel academically and personally, whether it's coming from family or themselves. This pressure can breed a fear of failure and a perfectionist mindset, where anything short of flawless is seen as unacceptable. This perfectionism, however, is a confidence killer. It discourages risk-taking and embracing new experiences, limiting your growth and learning opportunities. In the long run, it erodes your confidence and heightens anxiety. If you're the first in your family to study abroad, the weight of that responsibility can feel immense. And for many international students, studying abroad isn't just about education—it's about establishing a better life. That can make the pressure to succeed even more intense.

Social Anxiety and Fear of Negative Evaluation

Social anxiety can be another major hurdle for international students, further damaging confidence and self-esteem. Social anxiety is the fear of being judged, scrutinized, or negatively evaluated by others in social situations. When you're in a new cultural and social environment, that fear can be amplified. Many international students constantly worry about how they're perceived, and this fear can prevent them from fully engaging in academic and social settings. The result is a downward spiral of reduced confidence, increased fear, and missed opportunities. That fear of being judged or embarrassed can lead to unconscious mistakes, creating a self-fulfilling prophecy of failure and reinforcing feelings of inadequacy.

It's a tough cycle, but the good news is that awareness is the first step toward breaking free from it. It's important to remember that everyone's journey is different, and the comparisons you make are often unfair and unfounded. Focus on your growth, be kind to yourself, and take things one step at a time. Confidence, like success, is a process, not a destination.

OVERCOMING COMPARISON AND BUILDING CONFIDENCE

Acknowledge Your Current Accomplishments

As an international student, it may be hard to believe, but you already accomplished a lot, and it's time to give yourself some credit. You've made a bold move that not everyone has the courage or opportunity to make. Moving to a new country, especially at a young age, is a massive achievement in itself. The fact that you've taken this huge leap says a lot about your bravery and determination. Not everyone gets the chance— or the guts— to leave their comfort zone, immerse themselves in a foreign environment, and start building a life from scratch. So, if you're questioning your accomplishments, stop for a moment and acknowledge that you've already done something remarkable. Gaining acceptance into a university in another country is no small feat. Just because more people are doing it now does not make it any less impressive. The rigorous application process, the competitive nature of admissions, and the sheer determination it takes to move abroad—these are serious accomplishments. Just being here means you've shown a level of confidence, resilience, and adaptability that many people can only dream of. The boldness to leave everything familiar, the courage to trust yourself to build a life in a completely different place—that's a testament to your strength and belief in your potential. This leap of faith is the very essence of confidence, even if you don't always feel it.

Beyond making the move, what else have you accomplished? What are you naturally good at? What do your friends say you excel in? Write those things down. Keep a list of your strengths, skills, and accomplishments, and refer to it regularly. This isn't just a feel-good exercise; it's a way to reinforce a positive self-image and build your confidence. When self- doubt creeps in—and it will—that list will remind you of your worth and capability. You've done more than you think. Now, own it.

Building Confidence Through Reflection

Even if you're not feeling super confident right now, reflecting on the challenges you've already faced can work wonders. Think of every hurdle as a badge of honour, proof that you've got what it takes to handle adversity and still come out on top. Each challenge you've overcome is not just an obstacle in the rearview mirror; it's a stepping stone that has shaped who you are today. Recognizing this is key to building confidence. Ask yourself, "What did I learn from these experiences, and how can I use them as strengths?" That shift in mindset will allow you to see your challenges as skills you've acquired and assets you bring to the table.

The more you confidently articulate how you've navigated through tough situations, the more relatable and self-assured you'll become. You'll start to realize that you deserve every opportunity coming your way because you've earned it through grit and perseverance. So, when you find yourself in a room full of professionals—whether it's the CEO of Deloitte or a future boss—know that your journey, with all its highs and lows, gives you something valuable to offer. Maybe you learned a new language, cracked a tough financial puzzle, or aced a complex project; these aren't just achievements—they are testaments to your resilience and capability. Remember, your accent, race, or gestures are not a measure of the content in your mind or how smart you are. You know what you bring to the table, so confidently put it forward. Your experiences have equipped you with unique insights and strengths that are just as valuable as any other qualifications.

The Power of Affirmations

Affirmations are positive statements you tell yourself to reshape your mindset, especially when you're battling self-doubt or negative thoughts. They're like a mental reset button, pushing out the negativity and making room for positive beliefs. By consistently repeating affirmations, you can gradually shift how you see yourself and your surroundings, building both your confidence and self-esteem.

It's essential to start using affirmations early in your adjustment process. You'll notice that many international students who seem more confident or less affected by low self-esteem often come from environments where they've either been affirming themselves for years or had others around them regularly acknowledging their talents and accomplishments. These students are already primed to tackle challenges head-on, confident they'll succeed. But guess what? You can be that way too. The sooner you start affirming yourself, the faster you'll notice a shift in how you think and act. Here's the truth: confidence is a mental game. There's no challenge too big if you affirm yourself daily. And remember, whatever you confidently put out into the world will be received well. Confidence in how you present yourself is the key to being remembered, respected, and valued.

The Power of Visualizations

Now let's talk about visualizations. This technique is all about mentally rehearsing your success before it even happens. Visualizing yourself doing something that scares you—like asking a question in class, speaking up in a meeting, or attending a networking event— can do wonders for your confidence. Picture yourself handling these situations effortlessly. Imagine giving a flawless presentation where people understand you and applaud your insights. Visualize yourself solving problems, making valuable contributions, and receiving praise for your work. The more you do this, the more your mind begins to believe that success is inevitable.

Think back to the story earlier in the book. If the student had visualized her success before the presentation, she would have walked into the room with more confidence, ready to own the stage. Visualization is like mental training; it prepares your mind and body for real-life situations. It's the same principle behind practicing in front of a mirror—it's not just about going through the motions. It's about seeing yourself as confident so that, when the time comes, you naturally step into that role.

Practical Application of Affirmations and Visualizations

Here are some steps to apply these techniques into your daily routine:

- **Daily Affirmations:** Kickstart your day by reciting positive affirmations. Repeat things like, "I am confident and capable," "I am intelligent," "I can connect with anyone from any background," or "I am worthy of success." Don't just mumble through these—mean it! Throughout the day, whenever doubt sneaks up on you, go back to these affirmations. At the end of this book, you'll find a collection of affirmations you can use to guide you along this journey. But don't just rely on those—make them personal, make them yours.

- **Visualization Exercises:** Spend a few minutes each day imagining yourself succeeding in whatever challenges lie ahead. Close your eyes and picture every detail—whether it's acing that presentation, confidently asking questions in class, or effortlessly networking at an event. Don't just see it—feel the success. This mental rehearsal helps calm your nerves and builds confidence. If you need help getting started, there are great resources like guided visualization videos on YouTube. One I recommend is "Hour of Meditation" by Emmanuel Adewusi. This practice helped boost my confidence enough to write this book, and it can help you too.
- **Practice in Front of a Mirror:** Stand in front of a mirror and practice speaking or presenting. You'll see how you come across, giving you a chance to adjust your body language and facial expressions to exude more confidence. It's like a mini-rehearsal for real-life situations. Imagine you're talking to people from your class, club, or work, and practice making your points clearly and confidently.
- **Engage in Confidence-Boosting Activities:** Find what you're naturally good at and dive in! If you're a whiz at drawing, join a drawing class. If you're a tech genius, find a robotics club. By focusing on activities where you already excel, you'll boost your confidence in that area, and that positive energy will overflow into other parts of your life. It's all about finding your flow and leaning into your strengths.

Remember, by consistently affirming your worth and visualizing your success, you're training your mind to believe in your abilities. It's like sharpening a tool—you'll be prepared when you encounter challenges on your way. Combine this mental work with practical steps, and you'll be unstoppable.

Building Confidence Takes Time and Practice

Let's get one thing straight: building confidence is not an overnight process. As I've mentioned throughout this book, growth and development are gradual, step-by-step journeys. If you take a moment to reflect, you'll realize that you're not the same person you were five years ago—there's been growth, and that transformation didn't happen in one day. Some international students may find gaining confidence a bigger challenge due to their inherent personality traits or previous experiences, while others may naturally adapt with ease. The key is patience—confidence is not a one-time achievement, it's a journey that requires both time and effort.

Confidence takes practice

Building your confidence takes practice and lots of it. Affirmations and visualizations are great tools, but they're only half the battle. You need to back those up with real-world action. It's not enough to say, "I am confident"—you have to put that confidence to the test. Try to step into situations that make you uncomfortable, like networking events or social gatherings. These events allow you to step out of your comfort zone and measure how you interact with others and present yourself. Each time you push yourself to participate in these activities, you're doing the real work of building confidence. With every interaction, you're growing— learning to handle conversations, present ideas, and just be yourself in social and academic settings. It gets easier with time. It's a muscle you're building, and every time you use it, it gets stronger.

Chapter 8

The Final Word: Embrace the Journey

As you've probably realized while reading this book, adapting to a new culture is not a one-time event—it's an ongoing process. Today, you might learn something that shifts your perspective, and tomorrow, another experience may require a fresh adjustment. This cycle of learning, unlearning, and readjusting is key to thriving in a new environment. You'll discover that what works for one challenge may not work for another, and as society changes, you'll need to find new ways to stay ahead. You have to stay open and flexible so you can navigate the complexities of the transition more effectively, ultimately building a fulfilling life.

Learn to Take Risks and Seize Opportunities

Your university years are the perfect time to take risks and grab opportunities before the responsibilities of corporate life or family take over. Many international students come from more structured lifestyles, which can make it hard to see the opportunities around them. But this is your time—be open to discovering new passions and possibilities. Whether it's writing a book, starting a business, applying for internships, doing co-op terms, or joining clubs and competitions—do it now! Some risks may not pay off right away, but the lessons you learn will shape your future. By taking risks, you'll not only understand the society around you better but also experience rapid personal growth.

Plenty of international students started early, made connections, landed jobs, and are now steadily working toward their vision. While studying is your primary focus, don't miss out on growing your capacity and learning as much as possible. You're young, and time is on your side. Eventually, you'll become comfortable with discomfort because every challenge teaches you something new. These experiences will build empathy, humility, and a broader perspective, making you more effective in your interactions with others.

Consistent Effort, Accountability, and Erasing the Victim Mentality

As an international student, consistent effort and personal accountability are more important than just sheer perseverance. Many international students fall into the trap of a victim mentality, complaining about missed opportunities or feeling at a disadvantage. But here's the hard truth: maybe you're not putting in enough consistent effort, or you're not directing your efforts effectively. Learn to take advice from peers who know more than you, and apply it consistently. Consistency may not show immediate results, but over time, it builds momentum and progress.

Seek Mentorship

Mentorship is invaluable to your success as an international student. Meeting the right people and accessing the right resources can change your entire journey. Someone special once told me, "It only takes three steps to get to where you're meant to be." Often, just a few key connections can propel you toward your goals and greatly enhance your experience. Actively seek mentors who can provide guidance, support, and valuable insights. When I was in university, I was lucky enough to befriend someone two years ahead of me who constantly guided me and gave me excellent advice when I needed it. Mentors are your shortcut to navigating challenges and finding new opportunities. Don't underestimate their power.

Protect Your Mental Health

Adjusting to a new life can feel overwhelming, and sometimes it's okay to take a step back and breathe. Don't hesitate to take time for yourself or seek help, whether it's through professional support or a trusted network. Therapists can provide a safe space to unpack your feelings, help you develop coping strategies, and guide you through the process of unlearning old habits and adopting new ones. Journaling and self-reflection are also powerful tools to use when you're feeling stressed. Regularly writing down your thoughts, experiences, and emotions can give you clarity and help you grow from your challenges.

Never Give Up!

Giving up is not an option. Challenges are not the end, but redirections to better opportunities. You need to get up every day, dust yourself off, and keep moving forward. For example, if you don't do so well on a test, don't panic—reevaluate your study habits, join a study group, and figure out how to improve. Embrace every challenge, stay consistent, seek mentorship, and always be willing to adjust your mindset.

Remember, you're not just a student; you're a student of life. Every experience—whether positive or negative—shapes you, builds resilience, and prepares you for success. When you look back, you'll see how much you've grown, and trust me, you will realize how fulfilling and rewarding this journey can be.

Daily Affirmations for an International Student

1. I am an international student, and I am worthy.
2. I am an international student, and I am loved.
3. I am an international student, and I am where I am supposed to be.
4. I am an international student, and I am unique.
5. I am an international student, and I am smart.
6. I am an international student, and I am resilient.
7. I am an international student, and I am confident.
8. I am an international student, and I am fearless.
9. I am an international student, and I am good enough for that job. What I don't know, I can learn.
10. I am an international student, and I add value to every place I go.
11. I am an international student, and I am adaptable.
12. I am an international student, and I am intelligent.
13. I am an international student, and I am knowledgeable.
14. I am an international student, and I attract good people.
15. I am an international student, and I am not afraid to ask for help.
16. I am an international student, and I am a success.

17. I am an international student, and I am a winner.
18. I am an international student, and I am worth it.
19. I am an international student, and I can do anything.
20. I am an international student, and everything good will come.
21. I am an international student, and I thrive in every environment.
22. I am an international student, and I love my life.

www.ingramcontent.com/pod-product-compliance
Lightning Source LLC
Chambersburg PA
CBHW072215070526
44585CB00015B/1348